The Elsewhere Oracle

www.blacklawrence.com

Executive Editor: Diane Goettel
Cover & Book Design: Amy Freels
Cover Art: "The Penitent Magdalen" by Georges de La Tour (French, Vic-sur-Seille 1593–1652 Lunéville), ca. 1640, oil on canvas. Object Number: 1978.517. Gift of Mr. and Mrs. Charles Wrightsman, 1978.
https://www.metmuseum.org/art/collection/search/436839

Copyright © Michele Battiste 2025
ISBN: 978-1-62557-193-9

All rights reserved. Except for brief quotations in critical articles or reviews, no part of this book may be reproduced in any manner without prior written permission from the publisher: editors@blacklawrencepress.com.

Published 2025 by Black Lawrence Press.
Printed in China.

The Elsewhere Oracle

Michele Battiste

Contents

Near Elsewhere: A Prelude	vii
1. The Factory	1
2. The Gunsmith	3
3. The Mountain	5
4. The Barkeep	7
5. The Lake	9
6. The Orphan	11
7. The Ceremony	13
8. The Confectioner	15
9. The Soot	17
10. The Gardener	19
11. The Well	21
12. The Healer (Gloríana I)	23
13. The Ossuary	25
14. The Hunter	27
15. The High Street	29
16. The Immigrant	32
17. The Almanac	34
18. The Hermit	36
19. The Wolves	39
20. The Doctor	41
21. The Artifact	43
22. The Seer (Gloríana II)	45
23. The Storm	47
24. The Counselor	49
25. The Menu	51

26. The Robber Baron	53
27. The Compass	56
28. The Archive	58
29. The Sheriff	61
30. The Warren	63
31. The Plague	65
32. The Grave Keeper	68
33. The Teacher	70
34. The Drought	72
35. The Meadow	74
36. The Wildfire	76
37. The Council	79
38. The Pine	81
39. The Freeze	83
40. The Baker	85
41. The Moon	87
42. The Judge	89
43. The Spring	91
44. The Storyteller	93
45. The Trickster (Gloríana III)	96
46. The Torch Singer	98
47. The Ghost	100
48. The Farmer	102
49. The Woods	104
50. The Sun	106
Anywhere but Elsewhere: Coda	108
Acknowledgments	109
Art Attributions	111

Near Elsewhere: A Prelude

Once there was a mountain that everyone could see but no one could find. Those of us who lived in the valley towns along the range called it Mount Iron for its fabled veins, looted and abandoned. But cartographers would not label it on their maps, despite clear visual evidence of its existence.

The roads that led to Mount Iron skirted its base. Trails seemingly looped back on themselves, no matter how determined the blazer. Aspiring scientists attached transmitters to weather balloons and released them to air currents high above surrounding foothills, only to lose the signal once the balloons crossed the tree line. There are stories of those who disappeared in their desire to prove that their eyes didn't deceive them, but stories are stories.

It is the stories, however, that kept Mount Iron rooted in the landscape, fixed in our gaze. Adults told them to each other at night after the children went to sleep. Children told them to each other when they should have been sleeping. What was hidden near the summit. The woods filled with beasts. The perilous tarn, still and deep and fed by much more than snowmelt. A town, of course. Similar to our own towns, where we worked and lived, loved and slept and dreamt.

Occasionally, on clear evenings, when light silhouetted anything that rose above the horizon, we could see a thin stream of smoke rising from the backslope, and we worried that fire would cross the boundary that no person could. But we never saw fire, and the morning breezes carried no ash or scent of burning.

Our libraries hosted local and often amateur historians who spoke of a possible past that included mining, smelting, shipping away pieces of the earth cartload by cartload. It would explain, they said, the elevated levels of metal in our water, the century-old ordinance of raising our garden beds above the ground. No one much listened to the historians, though, as we stared out the window to a mountain that seemed more present than past.

This was, of course, all decades ago. When we were small. When we confused dreams with stories, stories with the goings on in our small lives. No one sees the mountain anymore. Other concerns hold our gaze: a dried-up river, dying pollinators, drought-fed wildfires that take out entire towns. The librarians now feature out-of-state lecturers who explain the impacts of vegan activism or boycotting monoculture.

I miss the mountain and its stories. The town, the lake, the woods, the people who could never leave. We kept them there. Haunted by our worries, not the other way around. We kept them there with our need to place our troubles elsewhere. With our need to tell our stories as if they belonged to others. As if we were not responsible. Not affected.

I remember the stories. These are our stories. My stories. Yours.

1. The Factory

If a structure	once existed in the forest.
If the owner	stood in the tower
	like a shooter flipping
	a coin.
If the insides	churned
	and processed way past
	3rd shift.
	If a road through
the woods	were grown over with shrub
	oak and sage.
If small children	swore they saw wisps of brown
	smoke while parents slept
	fitfully beneath the cold
	metal light of the moon.
If the sun	rose on a freshly settled dusting
	of soot each day.
If the barkeep	cursed each night that heap
	of dreck, that slag palace.
If tailings laced with arsenic, with cyanide, with mercury, with lead.	
If the dead	twined their bones
	about the roots of crooked trees. Then
	the factory.

Oracle

No structure is immune to the deterioration that comes with time. Buildings crumble. Dynasties collapse. Social norms slowly decline into irrelevance, like the traditional roles of breadwinner and homemaker. As structures fade or disappear, howevver, their legacies continue to shape our current and future worlds in unforeseen ways. For example, the coal-powered steam of the Industrial Revolution is a thing of the past, but we will contend with climate change for decades to come.

Internal structures can have similar impacts. Maybe the emotional defenses we developed to protect ourselves now hinder our ability to connect. Perhaps a familial role or a career path now feels like a prison. But we learn. We grow wiser and refuse legacies that we didn't choose. We fight to change both public constructions and constructions of the self.

It could be that you are in a place or period of flux—one where established structures that framed your identity are becoming outdated or obsolete. Maybe you are already creating or searching for new ones. Just know that impacts and influence of old structures linger. Don't be frustrated if you must contend with those impacts long after demolition. You have stamina. You will endure.

2. The Gunsmith

This town wants its feasts, but it's never eager
to dirty the kitchen. The judge and the sheriff prefer
our iron rendered for pots, never mind how we fill
them. The veins inside

                                the mountain. I dream they were liquid.
Not like blood. Like blackstrap molasses, a slow shadow
I can plunge an arm into. Pull out a dripping fist. I used
to work

        in a factory. Everything measured, neat
inside their molds, not even a thin spatter
of residue to scrape away. Now, the barrels from my forge
exhale smoke like

                 an unraveling, spent tendrils drift
and tangle. My husband said most things about me
should be hard, but I prefer silver to steel, earthworms
to rods, the scent of sweated leek

                         to a baby boar
chop, skin squeaky between teeth after the cook
scalds off the bristles. But this town
and their feasts. All tripe

                 and gristle, grease, wing.
I can barely watch the children stab at the meat, fat
trimmed ruthlessly and chucked into the woods.
The hunters come to me, specific in their desires.

Oracle

The violence of the gun may repel you, but the violence of the forge can be equally frightening. How can we anticipate the consequences of what we create? It may be time to bring into the world what you want but perhaps fear: a business plan, a poly-hearted love affair, a journey, a baby, a confession. You may need to break and remake your tools. You will risk a flawed product. There could be unintended fallout. And some cherished part of the self must shrink to make room for the part that is birthed alongside any new creation.

3. The Mountain

Blasted but not
stripped. Gold
gone. Silver
gone. Lead, zinc,
copper gone. Iron

abandoned. "Insufficient
quantities to merit
the expense of extraction."

The Council claimed
the tunnels and thin
anemic veins. Established
a perimeter, discouraged
collection of poppethead
remnants and chunks

of slag. Still, folks
linger. Wander the cart
tracks, marvel at the wrecked
spine and rusted
stakes. Under a full

moon the kids sneak
their way into the caverns,
bellow unnatural
sounds into space
made *something*

by loss, by what is taken
away. "Always something
left," says the smallest.
"Something for me."

Oracle

Reuse is a critical conservation strategy to protect natural resources. Thrift stores, consignment shops, garage sales, and swap meets help reduce the manufacturing and processing of raw materials. But reuse also requires creativity, seeing objects in a new light, understanding their potential, thinking of alternative purposes.

The value of reuse can be applied to aspects of our lives beyond possessions. What idea or ambition have you boxed up and stored in your metaphorical basement because it wasn't working? What shredded remnants of old relationships have you collected in your piece bag? Which passions have faded and been removed from display among your tchotchkes and bric-a-brac? What amazing things can you build from these discarded artifacts of your past? With whom might you share them?

4. The Barkeep

We keep our preachers
busy. The two priests, one rabbi, and Gloríana—
healer slash mystic slash midnight shifter at the gas station
on the corner of Pontiac and Catalpa—also have less

down time than they would like. It's not that the town
likes to talk. They just need assurance their stories
don't indicate an inner crookedness or irregular
heartbeat that marks them

uniquely wrong. They should know
better. We all know better: the accumulated
damage parceled out equitably
from here to the lake. The fallout
barely visible. Soot settles on each

of us. My rag water clouded
gray before the first pint is poured.
But we still speak of our wives
or bosses or children, how we accidentally sprained
someone's elbow or crushed a collection of antique
model airplanes in a rare but justifiable fit
of confounded rage. As if any confession could be

the worst of it. Up and down the line
of stools, hovering above the mumbling
and the sweating tumblers, the air fills then empties
then fills only with what can be forgiven.

Oracle

Confession is a sacrament in the Catholic Church. In Judaism, communal confession occurs before the Day of Atonement. Islamic confession is a direct matter between the individual and God. In the Church of Latter-day Saints, confession occurs during worthiness interviews prior to baptism. Confession is part of the fifth step of the Alcoholics Anonymous 12-step program. Criminals are exhorted to confess. Clearly, confession plays a significant role in many religious and cultural practices, but to what end?

What do you need to confess? More importantly, what are you hoping to achieve through confession? Forgiveness? Increased intimacy? Commiseration? Punishment? To assuage guilt? To cleanse your soul? Whatever the reason, confess what you need to confess. And know that whenever others confess to you, chances are they are standing in the shallows of their past, not swimming in its depths.

5. The Lake

Green like beginning (leaf primordium)
Green like promise (tangle of snakes)
Green like amulet (scarab's carapace)
Green like essence (secreted bile)
Green like riddle (hidden katydid)
Green like storm (tornado light)
Green like fortune (emerald vein)
Green like gamble (debtor's note)
Green like toxin (stem of foxglove)
Green like murk (understory)
Green like monster (from the shoreline)
Green like something soon to come

Oracle

To be superficial is to lack depth, to be concerned only with appearance. Superficial also implies a false appearance, to seem to be one thing on the surface until closer inspection. Green water lakes can be striking, often possessing a fairytale quality. Sometimes, when the light hits them, they emanate an otherworldly glow.

But their beauty can be deceptive. Green lakes are often choked with algae, which gives them their vibrant color. Fed by agricultural runoff, dense with fertilizer, algae blooms produce toxins and use up all the oxygen, killing fish and other aquatic life.

It is always easier to remain floating on the surface than it is to plumb the depths, but staying at the surface can give us a false sense of safety—even prove to be dangerous—when we don't know what lies beneath. Where do you need to take a deep breath and dive deeper? Into a relationship? A pattern of behavior? Your family's finances? Events in the past that you've blocked? You may already suspect what you'll find. Or you may discover that the monsters of your imagination are far worse than the monsters of the deep.

6. The Orphan

Records Sealed.[1]

Oracle

It is easy, and often preferred, to assign responsibility to others. Blame is buoyant and fun to fling about. There are some who find you an easy target to scapegoat, and sometimes all they need is your proximity to invent a poor turn of events and call you the cause.

On the flip side, assuming guilt has its attractions. To be guilty is to have power. To claim responsibility is another way of claiming control. You are not that important most of the time. Which is to say that sometimes you have grave responsibility and must wield it—and its impact on others—carefully. Other times, however, when the finger is pointed at you, go ahead and roll your eyes and turn away. Your energy is best spent elsewhere.

1. There were more of us once. When orphans
were a thing. After the war, the pandemic, the gypsy
killings, yadda yadda. Once we were emblematic
of a common, possible fate. No one hated us and we hated

only the lucky. That was before the town
started looking for sources of ruin, branded us
defective, more unsavory than tragic. Which is to say
we grew older, free ranging, exhibited signs of early

puberty. Our prime real estate rankles the Council—
the orphanage a Greek-revival holdover of civic
charity: a community that once took care
of its own. Our benefactor was wise

to the town's evolving priorities and adaptive
municipal processes. The row of catalpas obscure
a tall fence established the same year as the airtight
endowment. The staff are, for the most

part, caring and handsomely compensated. The smallest
orphans have the most say, and we developed
necessary efficiencies to handle a minder
we prefer gone. And we benefit, more often

than not, from excessive and anonymous kindnesses.
Hunters bring us fresh sausage and haunches. The older
children are favored with music lessons funded by donations.
I have chosen piano, and I am not in charge.

7. The Ceremony

In this place you are
between the gate
of ivory and the gate
of horn, not yet
undeniable.
> *Do not retreat I anoint you.*

In the light reflected
off the lake you are
a glint, possible
then figment then
possible then gone.
> *Do not evanesce I anoint you.*

You dart among
the aspen in the
mountain's shadow. Shiver
of leaves before
winter. Do
> *not still your limbs I anoint*

you. In the forest you
remain beneath
the roots. Do not
> *return there I*

anoint you. In this place you
> *are almost safe*

I anoint you.

Oracle

While everyone is an outsider sometimes (the new student, employee, or neighbor), some of us—the weirdo, the loner, the shy, the unstable, the beaten down—seem destined to haunt the perimeters of social circles. People who have been relegated to—or have chosen—outsider status often develop tenacity, resourcefulness, and keen powers of perception. They see things that others miss. They see through stories that others accept. That is their power, and through that power, outsiders can transform into an integral role, such as shaman or sage. While that role may still be relegated to the edges, it is the edges that define the shape of the group.

This may be a good time to examine your social, family and work circles. Perhaps you are feeling like an outsider and have underestimated others' esteem of you. Perhaps your good qualities are masked by defensive, self-protecting behaviors, creating a wall between you and those you'd like to be close to. Maybe you are dismissive of someone who could be a friend or an ally, or you've had a hand in making someone feel negligible or extraneous. A key element of group dynamics is that they shift. What direction do you want those shifts to take?

8. The Confectioner

When I was born, the world smelled
sour. Like the air had been vinegared
and left to stagnate in the sun. I cried
for sweetness. I would not
shush. My father, sleepless and near
hysterical, fed me honey

from his fingertips beneath
the table so the town would not think
he favored me above the others.
It was not out of love he kept me
sated. If he could have drowned
me in honey, he would have,
but there was never

enough. Even now, when he looks
at me, I see his desire to go
for the throat. Though I bring him
shards of toffee, caramels so
sticky they have unrooted
more than one tooth. He can't forgive
my escaping consequences

for a weakness I refused
to overcome. I am not undone
by sugar. Instead, the small
ones crowd my case to choose
chunks of fudge and nougat.
Bodi claims 21 brandied cherry
cordials every Monday morning
for their alchemic effect on
disorders of the heart.

Gloríana favors the ritual
consumption of marzipan in dark
chocolate before the Ceremony,
but none of this matters.
My father remains
disgusted, certain I shirk
the shared burdens
of Elsewhere. He is proof
that I do not.

Oracle

Love and hate have little to do with the desire for approval or the act of withholding it. Someone can love you and still feel the need to control, manipulate, or hurt you. They may even tell themselves that they are doing it for your best interests, to protect or improve you. They may be subconsciously protecting themselves from rejection or pain. And you can hate someone and still seek their approval, even though you tell yourself you definitely do not care what they think.

We can know this intellectually, but it's hard to know it in our hearts and psyches. We can do the hard work, make the difficult decisions, and repeat affirmations to help us understand our own worth and find approval from within. But still. The heart wants what it wants no matter how much we try to redirect its pulses. Perhaps the best way to preserve our fragile selves is to assume that approval exists without being communicated—to consider the communication apparatus broken, the message suspended unformed in the ether or badly damaged in the transmission.

And on the off chance that you are—consciously or subconsciously—the withholder, know that the power you gain from withholding is nothing compared to the power of sharing your pride, affection, connection, and understanding.

9. The Soot

The woods pretend to be the end
of things. Boles rot, fungus mottles
rock and stump, decay softens
the ground to a soggy carcass. What light
the overstory permits is tepid and littered
with spores. Children are warned
away. Hunters keep landmarks
in sight, carry long blades to hack
encroaching vines that sucker and stick.

The Council reluctantly
governs the ungovernable understory
that fills and overfills the stretch
between the mountain and the lake.
The hermit lives there. The beasts
we fear and the beasts we eat.
Gloriana's cures locked up
in tendrils and seeds. But beyond
the woods, the factory. From
the factory, the soot.

Oracle

What are you scared of? The dark? Strangers? The spotlight? Dying alone? Discovery of your secret fetish? A near-empty parking lot at night? Confronting what we fear can help us develop strength, foresight, and vigilance. But vigilance won't save you because the danger that will level you is not the one you anticipate.

Catastrophe blindsides us. Disaster is rarely foreseen. You can't figure out which threat will sneak past your safeguards. All you can know is that—despite your best defenses—something will get you someday.

It could be that you are expending so much energy keeping yourself safe that you are limiting your capacity to live. It may be time to take a risk that you find frightening. Or at least consider taking action. Remember that the choice to risk nothing is not without potential for disaster.

10. The Gardener

I dreamt the first garden once, lush and uncontained. Goats gamboled and nosed without stripping new kale or the tender tops of carrots. Peacocks napped with foxes, red pandas played with mink. Jeweled hummingbirds hovered tirelessly. Rain came, gently feeding streams that meandered through hidden caches of *squash and spinach and sweet pea and melon, beet and cucumber and peppers and sprouts.* The tree, unremarkable, was one of many. It bore forgettable fruit. Dark, I think. Sooty. It was not tempting but still I tasted. Nothing happened. Nothing needed to. We were simply left to do our worst.

Once, the extension rep suggested a ten-foot fence to prevent trespass. Deer, rabbit, squirrel. Plant the perimeter with mint and rhubarb, chive and fennel, enough garlic to choke a buck. Onions around tomatoes, mustard among the

Stake the dripline. Tie the net. But I don't begrudge the animals what they make off with. They give back what they get.

Oracle

The ideal situation is often ideal because it is unknown. We don't know its hidden blemishes, and we are good at filling unknown gaps with what we desire for ourselves. What we see: the couple that never fights, a colleague's cushy job, a rival's award, the friend whose social platforms blow up every time she posts. What we don't see: loneliness and lack of connection, invisible workloads and mental stress, late nights and savings spent on chasing accolades, addiction to the short-lived, throw-away attention of strangers. What we forget: those who look at our lives and covet what *we* have.

It may be that, right now, it's easier to covet thy neighbor's whatever than it is to contend with aspects of your life that are disappointing or banal. And that's okay. We can't be working on ourselves all the time. But don't fall into the sinkhole of comparison. It's never a fair one. There's no way that your reality can come out ahead when sized up next to imagined greener grasses. Instead, understand that what you see as ideal is actually a vision of what you want for yourself. Claim that vision and move toward it.

11. The Well

Sediment and lime scale
slow the pump. Water,
caught and stilled in fragments
of aquifer, takes
on the character

                    of rock.
Iron-stained. Calcium
hard. Brittle with arsenic
leached from soil 67
miles away. Joe Bodi abandoned

the back fields long
after the well showed signs
of drying up, the reach
of ditch water and pollinators
shrinking each season
until Bodi had no
choice but to roll
his shoulders and wrench
off the center

                pivot.
It isn't safe or easy
to locate, lost to an aspen
stand taking back
furrows root by creeping
rhizomatic root. The pump

still works, still sputters
out groundwater for those
thirsty enough or dirty
enough not to worry
about the other side
of the rotted
platform. Mostly hunters
hugging

        the tree line
or a feral pack of students
shoving the small one
first. Some say

        radon,
uranium. Some say small
decaying animals fouling
the well. A few say
nothing, suspecting something
else beneath the surface
that waits for whatever
wanders near the woods.

Oracle

No source of sustenance is infinite. Wells dry up, fields go fallow, friends turn away, pets sicken, idols fall. Always before we are done needing them. What remains are fragile and ghost-like structures. Memories. Shadows. The past. It can be difficult to leave them. It can be difficult to stop asking them to nurture and nourish us. But unrelenting need can turn our nurturers into something ugly and hateful as their only defense against our outgrown dependence. It's possible your overreliance on something or someone is threatening to ruin the both of you. Or it could be that you are the well without one last drop to send to the surface.

12. The Healer (Gloríana I)

Begin   with poplars   aspen   at elevation
    cottonwood   along the creek   poultice
    of leaf bud   tincture of bark   reduce
      a fever   lessen   muscle ache joint
pain   swelling that will pinch
       a nerve   lavender to soothe
  worry   betony if the worry   can't
    be soothed   yarrow   if the ache
    is in the tooth   or to substitute
bearberry if   bearberry   can't be found
for wounds   plantain also   good
     but better   saved for asthma
  allergies maladies of a woman's
  waning moon   cycle   paired
    with dandelion   to detox   promote
digestive   health   mint mixed with
   Oregon grape cures
     hangovers   elders treat
  lung   ailments   introduce bee
  palm juniper   rid the body
     of mucus   purslane   for disorders
of the heart   every day   I

```
gather what    the woods offer
         I do not   fear   wolves      the hunters
              the rare and otherworldly
           wildfire      it will be
the woods       that take   me     insisting
       what is   reaped   will be      replaced
    I know better       than most      what can
      and cannot           save us
```

Oracle

Some ailments are fleeting, some are chronic, but everyone hurts. We can become undone by pain, no matter its origin or type: physical or psychological, emotional or spiritual. In our ardent desires to be well and whole, we place our hopes in healers and their remedies. Unscrupulous profiteers exploit that hope, peddling panaceas and snake oil and harmful, misleading promises. Even legitimate medicines and therapies can fail us, and sometimes it may seem the only thing left to do is surrender to illness.

But health—in all its physical and metaphysical forms—is worth fighting for. Perhaps you are ignoring a nagging symptom, worried what you might find out. Or maybe a current remedy isn't working or working well. It could be the person who is providing your care is no longer on the right path. While doctors, therapists, healers, and counselors are experts in their fields, you are the only expert of your self—body and mind. It is time to evaluate the care you are receiving and to be relentless in securing the care you need.

13. The Ossuary

Bones of creatures before
the wanderers. Bones of wanderers
before the town. A collapsed

architecture. Animal
femur. Infant fibula.
Nested vertebrae in their canted

tracks. Circling. Circling.
Circling. Bones ancient
and unidentifiable. Sternum

like a palm frond. Scapula
like moths. Beneath
the steps, a shifting beach

of teeth, shoreline jagged
with incisors the length of a small
woman's foot. The father

knows which storm
cellar. The sister knows
which lock. No one knows

why the piles, why the altar,
why we need them
for what is to come.

Oracle

The body is ephemeral. But only if you think of it as a singularity—a distinct vessel containing the self. If you think of the body as an integral part of the earth and—by extension—the universe, its cells destined to break down and nurture new cells—loam, grass, trees, stardust—the body is eternal. And after death, our bodies continue to mean something to others. Both profane and sacred, bodies are laden with significance and myth and superstition. In death, your body is part of your legacy, your continuation.

So in life, your body is precious. Not for meeting aesthetic or athletic standards deemed culturally valuable. But because it is, simply, you in the material world. You can't predict the challenges your body will endure as it ages and evolves, the joys and pleasures it has yet to encounter. What is your body telling you? What somatic needs or desires have you put aside? Do not take your body for granted. Leave behind remarkable bones.

14. The Hunter

It is not brave to be
    necessary. Not potent
        to be an instrument
            of someone else's
        appetite. I shoulder
    my gun the same way
yellowed aspens quake

in a wind no one can
    feel. Throw my knife
        like an apple falling
            in the immigrant's
        orchard. Rabbit,
    pheasant, turkey,
dove. Transformed

by a twitched trigger:
    haunch and breast,
        wing and heart. When
            I walk in the woods,
        I move like a middle
    manager, safe in my
lack of authority.

The pack trails me,
    close in when I step
        off the path. Townsfolk
            shiver at the thought, as
        if the wolves were a
    threat. As if I were
worth their bother.

Oracle

There are jobs we do that we hate, but they are unavoidable and ours. Cleaning the toilet. Completing the expense report. Weeding the yard. Some of us choose to contract that work out: housecleaners, administrative assistants, gardeners. But some of us are the ones doing others' grunt work. All of us—at one time or another—take on a boss's, a partner's, a parent's, a child's distasteful or burdensome chores and find ourselves wondering—to quote a famous line in a famous song, "Well, how did I get here?"

While this type of labor may sometimes be necessary, other times we take on work we resent because of fictions we tell ourselves. That we aren't qualified for different work. That it is our duty. That the other is incapable. That it is better to shut up and do it than to risk conflict. That it is only temporary. The problem is, the more we do the work, the more we (and others) believe the work is ours. Think hard about your labors. It's possible that you have assumed someone else's responsibilities to your own detriment. And the resolution may be simply to stop.

15. The High Street

One Catholic, one Methodist, one Presbyterian church. The Apostolic spire—tapering to a savage point among the kestrels—resented by Protestants who stopped at modest steeples.

Grossman's Apparel and Dry Goods. Reliable stock of steel toes, cast iron, coveralls, alfalfa. Sabbath in the backroom every Saturday.

The statue at the intersection of High and Catalpa. Hand scrubbed each spring with stiff-bristled brushes. *Beloved Town Father* eroding from the plaque. More often referred to as *Evil Fuckwit* and *Ruinous Bastard*. As in, "Turn left at the Evil Fuckwit," or "if you pass the Ruinous Bastard, you've gone too far."

La Maison Bleue. Farm-to-table, forage-to-kitchen, slaughter-to-plate restaurant of some notoriety. Service can be uneven.

Elsewhere Public Library and Archives. Eighty-two shelves, fourteen cabinets, eleven overcrowded specimen cases filled with "variations on normal," and three rotating displays of mining, manufacturing, and agricultural achievements of local note.

The Stumble On Home: short-term
efficiencies and temporary
asylum. How their legs buckle
when they realize they belong.

Elsewhere City Hall and International Heritage Site.
Location of first Ceremony and final (supposedly) treaty
fairly (supposedly) dividing territory between the town
and those (of lore and local superstition) not of the town.

Creeper & Ivy Flower and Garden Shop. Specializing
in native flora resistant to alkaline groundwater
and attractive to pollinators. Serving gardeners
in compromised ecosystems.

The Odeon. Community productions of
Williams, Albee, O'Neill, Brecht, Ibsen, Miller.
Funded, primarily, by unadvertised
midnight shows of disreputable renown.

Elsewhere Savings and Loan (see statue).

Elsewhere Mining HQ and Company Store (see statue).

Bitter Greens Grocery. Wash all produce
before consumption. Wash skin in case
of contact. Wash all produce regardless of use.

Oracle

Home sweet home. Home is where the heart is. Home is where you hang your hat. There's no place like home. The idealization of home can make even the most pragmatic among us feel conflicted and full of angst. Rarely is home ever what we wish it to be.

At its best, home is a source of comfort, familiarity, and safety even when it is also the source of dysfunction, conflict, and a boatload of emotional triggers. At its worst, home is the least safe place. But we can't fully leave behind our homes even if we want to. They are part of our histories and, therefore, our identities. But how they shape us is within our power.

It may be time to examine the relationship between your home and self. What is it about your home life (past and present) that is affecting the way you show up in the world? Perhaps you can change your relationship to home. Perhaps not. But you can change the way home influences your perceptions, behaviors, and sense of self. Because where we come from is not who we are.

16. The Immigrant

No one chooses
Elsewhere. No one finds
themselves flanked by shrub
oak and hawthorn, ignoring
the one road
out. No tourist
shop to hold your
attention. No next town
over to send you
our way. The mountain—
blasted to bedrock
and dust—beckons no
feckless day trippers.
Rangers leave us
to the hopeful process
of ecology, shrinking
behind a line of firs planted
a century ago with unknown
motivation but clear
intent.

    I coax what I can
from stunted orchards:
peaches and apples
not good for much but mash
and cider. Melons in rows. Wild
berries from the woods, mulberries
at its edge, blueberries following

the rail from mineshaft
to factory, strawberries
in the shadowed interior
and I tell myself

I am not frightened
of much. I was a botanist
before Elsewhere, splicing
grape varietals and heritage
tomatoes. No one holds my
past against me. They don't
know anyone as strangers. Once
you're here, you're home.

Oracle

All of us feel trapped at some point. A job, a relationship, family, bitterness, a bad investment, habit, a hometown, a ghost town, financial difficulties, an inherited curse. Even success can feel like confinement—the "lives of quiet desperation" that Thoreau ascribed to days of joyless work to maintain the emblems of achievement and wealth: houses, farms, livestock.

Whatever your source of confinement, you may convince yourself that it makes sense to stay put. You may think that you can make it work and even be content, wrestling life from degraded soil. Perhaps you believe that staying is proof of your strength or courage or fortitude, that it is a prison of your own making and so you belong there, or that it is—at least—the devil you know. But every situation has an escape hatch. If you are not ready to wriggle out, crack it open to let in the light. The life that is on the other side will be there when you are ready.

17. The Almanac

What is to come: a mild
winter, murky spring. Lengthening
days that sputter   *one midnight to the next*
and stall. Rustling tree   *the limit of*
line on several windless   *arboreal growth*

nights. Plant beneath a budding
moon when waning crescent.   *alternative May moons*
Do not rush harvest. The first
frost will hesitate. Junipers
will encroach. Collect

piñons. Toast the meridian   *an imaginary semi-circle*
each time planets   *of sky arcing overhead*
cross. Jupiter will shine
as bright as the old gods.   *light reflected from a star*
A good year for Brussel sprouts,

the Perseids, Samhain. Postpone   *death-night of the old year*
ghost hunts, controlled
burns, dredging the spring. If air
stagnates, switch your pickling   *lacto-fermentation*
brine. The mountain will

erode endlessly. Autumn   *slopes erode to become more gentle*
will be eternal. Guard your time.   *less likely to collapse*

Oracle

What do we trust to intuition, and when do we go outside ourselves for guidance and signs? Considered either instinctual or unconscious, intuition appears to have an oppositional relationship to cognition. However, intuition is strengthened by conscious processes—learning, synthesis, reasoning—ingrained in our unconscious until we don't know how we know, we just know.

If you find yourself second-guessing your intuition, remember that it is not some mystic sixth sense. It is the grand accumulation of your knowledge and perceptions (as well as the accumulated knowledge and perceptions of your ancestors). See where it leads you. If it seems that your intuition has been recently taking you down the wrong path, it may not mean that you need to get more in touch with your inner self. It may be that you need to look outward. Do some research. Ask an elder. Take a class. Feed your intuition before you trust it. Then trust it. This is no time for self-doubt.

18. The Hermit

I was told there was
a brother—a babe
so winsome he broke

all the institutional rules
of emotional and demonstrative
restraint. He went

quickly while I—already
pallid with a feral sense
of our predicament—

lingered. Years
passed. The prefect risked
harsh discipline to tell

me the world into
which I'd soon be
discharged held one

prize. *Claim him.
He couldn't have gotten
far.* And she pinched

hard the underside
of my arm as was her fashion
of encouragement. I left

the orphanage. Walked straight
to the wooded edge
of town. Like all

orphans, I held a certain
fondness for tall trees
at the borders. Like

all orphans, I have
always lived between
two worlds, but now

an anchor leashed me
to one. It was a strange
liberty, knowing no matter

how deep I went, the fact
of a brother would insist
on a world outside

the woods. The line between
us slack but always
the promise of a sudden
tug. That kind of certainty

makes a man brave and
foolish. Waiting.
Patient.

Oracle

We all need something to rely on. The world is a scary place; imagine how scary it would be without a safety net. Whether yours is woven of family, friends, savings, faith, an insurance plan, a cache of apocalypse food, favors owed, the government, or a mélange of resources, it's important to have a source of security, something to fall back on when everything else falls apart.

But healthy dependence relies on reciprocity. We must nurture and take care of those people, things, or beliefs we hope will take care of us when we need them the most. There's a chance that someone who depends on you is neglecting you. More likely, however, you may be taking a source of support or connection for granted. Without your care and attention, it will languish and lack the strength to boost you up when you need it.

19. The Wolves

                Some say they went away but they
            did not. Some say—with anger
      and hostility—they return to
our lands, but that is based
      on a false premise: that the
            wolves are not the land. That
              the woods would have ever

            given them up. They
         have lingered like we have
   lingered. They claimed
the forest like we claimed
    the mountain. They have eaten
        very few of us. We argue
          viciously among ourselves

            and the Council once mentioned
          extermination as if that were
an option. As if the wolves
were made monstrous by
    nature and not our fears.
        As if the hunter did not love the
            like better versions of himself.

Oracle

To have an enemy is to identify ourselves—at least partially—through an oppositional framework. What we are not. What we hate. What we are against. To have an enemy also gives us—at least some of us—purpose.

Not necessarily to ensure our own victory, but to ensure their defeat. Even if it means we lose a little. Or a lot. To have an enemy narrows our thinking, as we prioritize information that confirms our biases or justifies actions that we would otherwise abhor.

At the same time, to have an enemy empowers us, demands strength and fortitude (that we perhaps did not know we had) to defend what we love or what we believe. We can offer grace and honor to an enemy, fighting them without villainizing them (and, in the process, villainizing ourselves). If you are in conflict with someone, maybe it's time to stop thinking about winning and losing. Maybe it's time to think about what you are fighting about, what's at stake, and what outcomes you want. This might be different than defeating your enemy and it might change your battle plans. Or it might reinforce them. Fight on.

20. The Doctor

As one comes to understand from various and objective news
stories about chronic inequities endemic to our medical system,

rural and remote communities suffer disproportionately from the lack
of medical professionals who are, understandably, less inclined

to practice outside of cities where, on average, salaries are higher,
opportunities are greater, advancement is accelerated, and quality

of life is incomparably better (as evidenced by lifestyle
magazine rankings presented in enumerated lists). Which might

lead one to believe that doctors who practice in small, far-flung,
difficult-to-locate, undetected-by-GPS towns are inferior

to their metropolitan counterparts. And if visited by an urbane—
and most certainly hypothetical—adventurer sporting microfiber

and moisture-wicking wristbands complaining of decreased
performance and sore tendons after a barefoot 10K of his own design,

I would have little to offer other than a poker face, a prescription
for a sound pair of sneakers, and a bill for wasting my time. However.

When faced with proximal lightning strikes, crushed limbs or digits,
embedded barbed projectiles, ingestion of unknown toxins, unidentifiable

bites, not to mention byssinosis, silicosis, mesothelioma, worms, and the common croup, I would bet on a brighter prognosis

and better chance of exceeding it by seeking treatment at my office rather than those of my urban peers. As if anyone here has a choice.

Oracle

Relativism can crush anyone's self-esteem, but that's only when your basis of comparison is entrenched criteria most likely skewed to privilege existing power dynamics. Who says money is worth more than art, position more than kindness, beauty more than sharp, cunning wit? Perhaps those who benefit from traditional (and therefore biased) value systems? Combined, your skills, talents, and knowledge are incomparable. Powerful. Imperative. Worthy of envy and awe. If that is difficult to accept, it is time to stop measuring yourself by the inadequate and incomplete metrics of others.

21. The Artifact

If patterns can be detected
from what others leave behind, this artifact is a
variation on normal. (Deviation, of course, establishin
g while narrowing parameters of normal.) Striations on the
surface of the artifact are above standard, but the source mate
rial is coarse and easily eroded. Which
placing under scrutiny those who held it.
Those who let it go. Those who examine the artifact,   in pla
ces it is   translucent, are best served holding it up to the light
Someone dug the artifact from th
e ground, thinking perhaps he found a coin or an offering from plag
ue times. A child's token. A healer's charm.
He knew instinctively it came from the lake whe
n the lake swelled and churned beneath storm clouds,
brought to the surface what rested at its depths. For th
at reason, most members of the city council rejected the a
rtifact,   the most benign ethnogra
phic studies with rigorous but un
founded denials of
credentials. No one
trusts the
city cou
ncil. Ev
ryone
covet
s the a
rtifact.
Belie
ving it
the
secret of   remain.
of Else   hy   we
wh   of   w
e   ory
r   e st
e, th

Oracle

Some of us seek answers in science, some in various versions of God, some in empirical observations and experience, some in the past. Wherever we seek answers, know that the knowledge held there is partial, the stories only a few of many, and its space more mystery than fact. If you are searching for an answer, remember no source is infallible or complete. What you are looking for may be in a place you would never think to look.

22. The Seer (Gloríana II)

True   there is a   midnight
    blue   velvet curtain   crystal
    beads threaded   on   delicate
        floss draped   across
the altar   a sphere
        of quartz   cloudy
with impurities   glinting   back
    candle   flame   one bright
ember   of frankincense
        its languid   reach of smoke
    smelling   holy or   vaguely
        resurrected   silk slung
    over   windows half-obscuring   views.
The lake.   The woods.   The factory.
    People believe   what they find
    easy   to believe   they ask
me to show   what lies
        beyond this   town, this   job, this
year, this   sin, this   suffering but I
do not   show them.   I shake
    or nod my   head   flutter

```
    my eyelids      trace
  veins     in their arms
with my finger      tell them
        what they  show me.
```

Oracle

People see what they want to see, but what do they reveal? We all make choices about how much of our inner selves we share and with whom. Share too little and people will become wary of the veneer. Share too much and others can be discomfited by unearned intimacy. It's difficult to balance authenticity with etiquette, vulnerability with composure.

But what parts of our selves do we reveal without knowing? Which bits leak out, exposing our weaknesses despite our best efforts to seal the cracks. And to whom? Sooner or later we all let something slip. Some people are perceptive and gentle with the discovery of others' secret selves. They can be wonderful friends, advisors, and mentors. There are those, however, who prey on slippages, unintended disclosures, misplaced confidences. It may be time to hone your powers of self-awareness and determine what of your barest and most tender self you are sharing and with whom.

23. The Storm

Like a crone calling home her dim
                    strands of memory, weaving back
loose threads of something still

                            unraveling, the storm gathers then
        collapses. Gathers. Collapses. Always
            above the lake. The sky bitter with chill. The water—

            murky with decay—warm. The difference
                    pulls filaments of mist into air where
            they pool like blood in a bruise.

                People fidget. Snap at dogs and
                    persistent children. The pressure too
                  much, the breeze out of balance. Then

                        the sound of something
                          striking.
                            Then

      release.

Oracle

Some of us put a lot of mental energy running through potential scenarios in order to be prepared for anything. Some of us put energy into observing our environments, so we are good at understanding cause and effect. Some fantasize about endings as a way to imagine new, implausible beginnings, and in doing so, come to understand the future we approach. And most of us know that person who always predicts what comes next in every story or movie, recognizing narrative seeds and how they grow, both above and below the surface.

We don't always see the signs, but when we do, that's only the half of it. Randomness—the potential for unknown factors to change a trajectory—is stronger than our powers of deduction or insight. It's possible that change is imminent, or an event is on the horizon, and you are getting prepared. You may even be the catalyst. Just remember that there are factors beyond your control that can change the path forward. Be ready to shift, to pivot, to go to plan B.

24. The Counselor

Let me make something
clear. I am not
muscle, not the swagger
of persuasion, not a glinting
lure. I have been

told a lack of conviction
in my posture sets creatures
at ease. Such a sparsely
populated town requires
a person of inadequate
vision to miss the potential
in others, and in that way

I am gifted. Some people I can
barely see and some are just
the sound of wind moving
through a hastily abandoned
house, small objects
skittering in dust. I do
my best to keep them

here despite their apparent
lack of substance. They could
leave if they chose, cross
the same way a child skips over
a sidewalk crack. But they think

they are part of the slag
and seepage, chemical
green water, ulcered
ground. This is my skill.
Suggesting we were once
counted among
the consequences.
Insisting nothing
has changed.

Oracle

It is easy to see the flaws in others, to know how they could improve not only their relationships (particularly with you), but also the ways they move through the world. If only they would control their anger, learn to trust, try to understand, stop drinking, develop empathy, listen, work harder, believe in themselves, _____ (fill in the blank). We often think the best way we can help them is to help them fix themselves. What we often forget is that others feel the same way about us. They see our flaws. They know exactly how we can be better.

If you are struggling in a relationship, you may be expending too much energy focused on what is wrong with the other. When we focus on the flaws of the other, we forget our own. When we try over and over to get them to hear us, we aren't hearing them. If you keep running up against a wall in a relationship, try turning your attention and energy inward. It may be that for anything to change, you need to start with yourself.

25. The Menu

The kitchen of *La Maison Bleue*
makes do with what the woods

                        Hors d'oeuvres
                        Escargots á la Bourguignonne
have to offer. Sous chefs woo
hunters, hunters track
                        Duck Pâté en Croûte
waitstaff trailing a scent
of intrigues and grudges,
affairs and abandonments.
                        Soupe Aux Champignons
Guests can guess the specials

                        Les Plats Principaux
from the rotisseur's slump
before his block, gesturing
with the crushed limb
                        Lapin á la Moutarde
of a small carcass;
or the saucier's manic
stirring, tomatoes falling
                        Civet de Sanglier
to pieces in the fat of wild
boar. The sommelier
erases wine   *Chateau Margaux*
from the slate,
whispering nothing
is left but the stag   *Venison Bourgoinon*

her ex-lover killed,
but it is unfit for such
a fine pairing.

Les desserts
Macaron
Madeleine
Clafoutis
Crème Brûlée

Oracle

Despite vast swaths of poverty and deprivation across the U.S. and the world, we have evolved to a point where we problematize—and even pathologize—abundance. "Decision fatigue"—the phenomena in which having too many choices makes us tired, unhappy, and unable to choose—is a real, albeit recent, malady. Which is why the concept of curation is gaining popularity. Playlists, Netflix collections, the top 25 books of the year, this season's must haves, and the power foods no diet should be without all provide choices with limits. Someone, or some algorithm, has done the culling for us.

It's important to remember, however, that when we choose among options offered to us, someone else has pre-determined what matters. And they make those determinations with their own agendas and biases.

It's possible you have an important choice to make. Just remember, the best choice may be the one not offered. It may be the one someone else discarded. It may not show up on any list.

26. The Robber Baron

I love them by the dozens, itty
bitties and big ones. They swarm

the grounds, tilting always slanty
toward the fence. Scrappy up

the catalpas for a view. Higher
is worth more. Highest is worth

claw and tooth. I love it
when they grapple, fling another

down. I tell the hunters, *bring
them meat!* I tell the lawyers,

ironclad the deed! I tell
the teachers, *more music!* Make

them softer at the edges, blunter
instruments, last them longer.

Funny little big ones all, some
making in my image, the parents

all gone. Myth has it into the woods
gone. The fact is not so easy.

Isn't that the case of every
orphan? A bit of myth, a bit

of fact. They shriek like so many
birds guarding their trees. *My*

tree, the orphans shout. I say
to the lawyers, *my trees,*

my assets, my orphans running
the garden paths always

to the fences, never to the gate.
Big and little ones love what

they know and what they know
is safe. I made this

town, stick and brick and storefronts
and asphalt. Smokestacks and

mosses. Bones in the ossuary.
Bones in the woods.

Oracle

It is reassuring to think identity is self-defined. We are who we say we are—revealed by *our* actions, words, and deeds. We are the choices we make, the options we reject. We imagine our selves, and we transform our selves into that image. We want to change and then we succeed. Or we fail. Even if we indulge in self-hate or self-pity or self-blame, we believe the "I" is the driver. The "I" is in control.

But our loved ones, those who care for us, those we admire and those we despise, people who have harmed us and people we have harmed—they all play a role in shaping our identity. We can try to control their impact on our lives, to limit their power, but even in those efforts, we play out their influence.

Right now, someone may have an outsized influence on your identity, and by extension, your fate. It's best to figure out who that someone is, and if you can't (or don't want to) limit their influence, you should at least understand its impact.

27. The Compass

You
do not have
to be certain. To the
west? Always mountains.
But three degrees south? Maybe
needlegrass tangled with wood nettles.
Maybe a two-lane backroad slow

with hills you can't			Once you disregarded
see past. Once you charted		true north. Once you
the migrations of painted		called every star the same
ladies and monarchs, intent		secret name so you would
on following their paths		not have to choose.
south until the waves		You do not have to
broke at your feet.		choose. You do not

have to navigate the bright and
absolute cardinal points. Look
away from the needle and
spin the way children
do. Whichever way
you turn, you are
here.

Oracle

There are times when the advice of others will steer us in the right direction and guide us to sound decision making. To put our faith in the wisdom of others, however, excludes a vast source of knowledge: our own.

Whether from experience, intuition, or study, our own insights hold as much—or more—weight as those from family, mentors, colleagues, teachers, and friends.

Whatever quandary or crisis you are facing right now, do not disregard what your intellect, body, and heart are telling you. Listen to others, weigh their words, and then follow your own compass.

28. The Archive

This transcript was discovered behind the pastedown of the foreman's logbook. Notice the dignified script, most likely his wife's. She married for a passion that gripped just long enough for consequences before a slow and inexorable evanescence.

The logbook documents the foreman's casual and systematic graft, how he skimmed workers' anemic wages under the guise of a residential tax. Some say that most orphans in town descend from him.

This epic was carved into railway ties in between the arrivals and departures of the Union Pacific. The narrative grew inversely proportional to the decreasing rail traffic as the mountain's last veins were tapped. The splinters are brutal and stubborn. Wear gloves.

This story was wrapped around several pinecones during a mast year, then buried. Many took root, grew haltingly. *The story is difficult to hear on still evenings. The story is difficult to decipher in the wind.*

Some say these pictographs etched on chunks of slag (and one misidentified meteorite) divine a different Elsewhere. Notice the storm clouds, the almost impossible translucence of the lake, how glassy, how underneath the water, the labyrinth draws you in.

Official population records occupy one whole (though narrow) shelf. The practice of recording only deaths began this last decade then stopped. Then nothing but pressed alyssum and small unidentified blossoms that were once blue.

An anonymous benefactor donated this collection of plaster casts that mended broken limbs. It seems that falling from trees was a regular thing among orphans. Note the scrawled signatures, the notes of well wishes, the savage undertones.

Kept behind glass, our collection of scrimshaw represents an unusual engraving technique; verses hidden along tree limbs, in the outline of the mountain, in paving bricks that pattern High Street. Nursery rhymes, perhaps, but not appropriate for any child not an orphan. The bone is terrestrial. There has been an analysis. We await results.

These transcriptions are comprised of 756 recordings of the VFW's monthly open mics. The scrivener—most likely bored with the task of transcribing—applied a *bricolage* technique to mold a story about a torch singer who led her love to the edge of the lake and returned alone but not despondent.

This book belongs to schoolchildren who have prohibited any adult from turning a page. The children crowd around its covers, stare with unnatural focus and giggle lasciviously. Adults move quickly to the back room.

This sacred codex is for the dead. We tend to like them more than the living who behave like frightened ghosts fading into the landscape.

This story doubles as a cipher, but no one has discovered an encrypted text it can decode.

This primer instructs our smallest citizens on the dangers peculiar to our town. Those who do not hone their skills of perception and reflex fare poorly.

This story continues being written. No one knows by who.

Oracle

Stories are power. Stories conjure and preserve. They create history, identity, and legacy. They influence the future. They precede us and then linger, like a fragrance, but also like essence. They have lives apart from us, reflecting us and on us, morphing and changing, shaping who we are in an endless process of becoming.

Who is writing your story? Who is telling your story? Recording it? Remembering? It could be that you are disconnected from your own story, missing the chance to learn from it—and, by doing so—to change its arc. Or maybe you are trying to hold on to it too tightly, and it has atrophied. Perhaps you are obsessively reliving your story, incapable of moving onto the next chapter. Sometimes what our stories need most is a healthy dose of neglect. Sometimes what we need most is to hear our stories from someone else's mouth. Chances are, you need to change your relationship with your story—and its writers, tellers, and recorders—to access its power.

29. The Sheriff

Some nights my face goes numb watching
over four blocks of High Street and a wilderness
of yearning. Everyone here wants

to be elsewhere. Spring-loaded
like children old enough to expect
monsters around every blind corner
but too young to do much
about it. They don't
remember the blight
behind us. Hollowed out

mountain. Tailings littering the woods. A water
table so suspect we treat rain like it's holy

water. I flush delinquents from the square, bust
up a skirmish now and then at the VF. Keep my finger

on the safety in case the past gets
restless, finds it way forward to take us
down for good.

Oracle

While the role of protector is often assumed through conscious choice (the decision, say, to become a parent, a counselor, or police), the drive to protect is primal. We protect what is ours reflexively, amygdalas in overdrive, responding to threats before our brains can consciously identify danger. Sometimes, though, we feel the urge to protect that which isn't ours—the vulnerable, the scared, those without recourse, those without power, those without voice.

Maybe you're a protector of animals, nature, immigrants, reproductive rights, small businesses. Maybe you watch over your elderly neighbors, an anxious colleague, the house finches that made a nest in your hanging plant. You might not have a full understanding of what the dangers are or where they are coming from. This may be a good time to reassess threats. And if you wonder if you have what it takes to keep what—or who—you love safe, don't worry. When the time comes, instinct will do its work.

30. The Warren

Rabbit in mustard sauce rabbit
stew rabbit in a Riesling jelly
rabbit *bourguignon* grilled garlic
rabbit rabbit *cacciatore* rabbit
ragout with *soppressata* and
pappardelle rabbit braised
in wine.

      Every living thing
has its predator, even if it's simply
time. The rush of death toward the warren
takes many shapes: coyote, fox,
peregrine falcon, but none so efficient
as *La Maison Bleue*, its bored
patrons, iron-poor and soft
about the gut.

      Each litter smarter
than the last, one more clutch
of fear bred into instinct. Avoid
the wild thyme and emerging
clumps of chive in the high, lonely
meadow: proximity of snares,
prey

    by association. Tunnel
deeper in the forest, aim toward the lake.

Oracle

Sometimes the fates are out to get us. Or God is out to get us, or the world, our neighbors, the Man, debt collectors, our ex, the undertow, human resources, high cholesterol, or the sheer bad luck of a confluence of catastrophes. Threats to our health, happiness and prosperity are everywhere, seen and unseen, dire and minor, imminent and evolving. It can feel like too much. And sometimes the fight feels already lost.

But fortune favors the innovative, the resourceful, the strategist who does not abandon the fight but rather switches tactics. This may be a time when your methods of survival and success need to evolve. Replace an evasive maneuver with an assertive parlay, or vice versa. Refine your skills of persuasion and influence. Strengthen your network of support and your relationships with allies. Apply your expanding store of knowledge to closely held assumptions. Whatever you do, don't give up.

31. The Plague

It came slowly.
    Some could not be saved.
Its broken gait
heralded damage
but no one thought
    Some sunk. Or shrank. Or caved
    in. Insides failing,
to prepare. It grew
    unknowable. We gathered
    on corners as if waiting for
louder. Bigger. Filling
silences between
    a procession, pushing children
    to the front for a better
    view. The littlest ones fared
    best but witnessed
us. The air smelled different. Emptied
    too much. Learned
    to wrench their wrists
    from a stiffening grip.
then filled with suspicion and
    Some could still
    walk, made their way to the
disease. The factory smoke
slowed then stopped. Shouldered
aside by fear and its feral
    edge of the lake carrying
    what they could—a ring, a
stink. Shafts in the mountain
left hollow. Picks and

                    ribbon, a letter. We buried
spades rusting where they were
dropped. A few stood
                    them there. Beneath
their ground awkwardly,
as though to confront a phantom
                    rocks. Learned to
                    dread the heavy
                    rains. Wolves
they did not believe in, that
                    howled in the forest. Whoever
believes itself not dead. It had no purpose. It did
                    was left did
not linger. It did
                    not hear them.
not have to.

Oracle

Catastrophe is seldom a solitary experience and never an equitable one. Pandemics can take out an entire family while leaving another untouched. A hurricane decimates one community, and a neighborhood five miles away merely tolerates the inconvenience of downed power lines. A struggling small business declares bankruptcy after a four-day blackout, but the chain store around the corner has the resources to outlast the setback. One zip code is designated a superfund site; a code one digit away never worries their water may be poisoning their children.

But something that happens to one of us happens to all of us. Impacts ripple out like a contagion, literally and figuratively, and we are fooling ourselves if we don't acknowledge that the fallout lands everywhere. If you have suffered catastrophe, hopefully you have been lifted up by networks of support, empathy and aid. It may be time to give back. If you are suffering now, it may be time to ask for help or to access available resources. If you have yet to be touched directly by catastrophe, it can be difficult to recognize the need for your philanthropy, time, or energy. But people near you need your help as you, one day, may need theirs.

32. The Grave Keeper

More dirt than flesh, more root than bone. Rocks work their way up, appear like a child's treasure poorly hidden in the grass. I have no regard for ghosts or the secret, repressed obsessions they take to the grave. More partial to metamorphosis: this grass, this dogwood, this unruly patch of alyssum and blue mustard *is* the beloved brought back to life. Some souls refuse to change and wander the edges of the graveyard, forgetting the names of flowers and keeping a wary eye toward the woods. I am gentle with my trowel and dibber, my rake and secateur, my rudimentary botany and basic grasp of physics: what cannot be created or destroyed, what can only be transformed.

Oracle

Sometimes we're so preoccupied with who we are—with knowing ourselves and our truths—that we miss opportunities to transform. Or we see the opportunities, but they frighten us, so we reject them. Self-awareness and self-knowledge are critical, but so is negative capability—the ability to be comfortable with—to stay with—the unknown and to be receptive to what it brings.

If we cling to what we know about ourselves, insist on our strengths and weaknesses, focus on a single vision of the future or the defining influences of our past, we remain stagnant and grow stale. We become known to others by our most entrenched qualities—caricatures of ourselves.

Uncertainty and the unknown are doorways to growth and transformation. To walk through those doorways is to take a risk, and it may be that you are standing before such a doorway right now. While there are many factors to consider before walking through, don't let fear be one of them. And if there's no doorway in sight, maybe it's time for you to build one.

33. The Teacher

The small ones hunch, eyes scanning
from window to door to window, archiving
all ways out. Sometimes they howl. Sometimes they dig
their fingernails into their desks, smearing

the wood with blister juice and blood. They plead
for the hollowed-out mountain, reach for the soft
underside of my arms, pinch when I hold
them still beneath a ceiling lower than anything

else they know. They woo me with their talk
of starless skies, the invisible hum of bees
hived in the crags, but I've seen
their feet, the jagged scars, the dank cuffs

of their dungarees, the whiff of scum
and lake. Did you drink the water, I ask them, half
wild with woods inside my bones. They strike
me. Did you drink the water? Did you drink?

Oracle

The target of our anger is often not its cause. Perhaps the boss blames you for his own incompetence. You listen silently to the upbraiding and then yell at a cashier-in-training at the grocery store. You pretend to ignore your mother's cutting remarks on the phone. Then you hang up and treat your lover or friend to a similar dose of insulting snark. It's called displacement.

Chances are that a recent or ongoing occurrence of displaced aggression requires your attention. If you are the one acting out, know that there are larger forces at play—a situation or person you don't feel safe confronting. Use your energy to tackle the problem instead of attacking people who don't deserve it.

If you are the object of someone else's displaced anger or frustration, it may be harder to recognize, but you don't have to. Just know that no one gets to be mean to you. Take your ball and leave. For the moment. Or forever. And if the power differential is such that you feel like you can't take action (a parent, supervisor, teacher, for example), find help.

34. The Drought

Some say   act of God some   say
the sky is doing   its best
       to be rid of us   our mad
digging   picking smelting   felling
the Earth   gouged beneath our
tools and who   knows what our geniuses
will dream   up   when we turn
      our gaze to clouds and see all
that unmined   potential

                       the sky
backs away   takes what water it can
    safeguard   during our anthropogenic
tantrum   you   can see rising
tempers in   the brutal   clench
    of jaw   the municipal   frenzy
when the lake   sinks the creek   slows
    to an ooze   watermark high
on the bank   scum hardening   fields
  in the distance turned   to stubbled
tinder   the woods   tinder   houses
  tinder   tempers   tinder   wind
        wicked   with fuel

     and the sky   still
    retreating   dark and sodden and laboring
with waiting   until we've worn
    ourselves   out limp   and heaving
then the sky   waits some more

Oracle

It can be difficult to watch others make mistakes. It's especially difficult when we know that we'll be the ones helping to pick up pieces or make things right. We can offer guidance and try to steer loved ones down a different path, but in the end, we bite our lips and stand aside when they adopt a kinkajou, tell the boss what they really think, or go on a two-week road trip with their mother.

There are times, however, when we need to interfere—when we are morally obligated to prevent harm. It could be as simple as taking a drunken friend's car keys. It could be as complicated as working to change local and state laws that regulate industrial waste. It could be risky, like blowing the whistle at work or reporting a neighbor for suspected abuse. If the time for action isn't now, it could be the right time to practice the skills needed to speak out. Sooner or later, we all are faced with the responsibility—and the challenge—to step up. We are more likely to do it if we are prepared.

35. The Meadow

                                        Sheath
and blade. Minute serrations, seed head the same
beginning whether named inflorescence or spike.
The spikelet, its awn, rachilla, and glume. Even
the stolon. Even the apex and leaf

                                          primordium.
Countless tall grasses. Exceptional drought. How we
can't resist crushing the brittle stems. How little
we know about fuel when it's not in service to us.
We pine

       for the flash of fireflies. We believe
a semi-arid landscape can't sustain a meadow but it
can. There is surface enough. And seed. Remember
the spikelet. Remember the awn

                                   and the glume.
And if the grass burns hotter and longer than you
ever thought possible from one hunter's careless
spark, remember the warren and run.

Oracle

People often think of nature in two ways: something to be exploited or something to be protected. Both mindsets perceive nature as a resource: it feeds us, holds the secret cures to diseases we haven't yet experienced, provides the water we depend on, yields oil and wood and minerals and metals that build our cities and power our industries. It serves as an asylum for our souls, inspiration for our art. But we can't forget about nature's power, its potential to create and destroy with no regard for humankind.

Similarly, no matter how you are perceived by others for what you can or cannot offer, you have power and potential to create and to destroy. Others may try to dissuade you of this. They may try to convince you that you are only as good as what you give them, possibly while denigrating what it is that you are able to share. But don't be persuaded. Beneath your surface is a seed of great strength, force, and change. You make things happen.

You may be at a crossroads. Or a dead end. Or a breaking point. You may choose to plumb your reserves of power, or your power may rise up in a great involuntary wave in response to provocation. It is at this point you have a crucial decision: create or destroy. Either way, make it beautiful.

36. The Wildfire

Imagine how alive—the surge

> of woodland creatures
> ahead of the creeping
> fire line, their racing
> electric with panic and how

we root for them and believe

> every spark and tinder
> escapable, the alternative
> (flame creeping in from all
> sides) unimaginable.

So we picture the dead

> wood, the charred
> soils, the blackened
> stone all smoldering
> in the aftermath. That

we can sacrifice. That is what
we are willing
to include in the possible,
not a fire

> that ends it all. So mice
> and mountain lion reach
> the lakeshore, bright

green shoots will push
through the char, and
as night deepens the red,
the glow, the flickering, we nod
imperceptibly at what we can't stop

knowing. The burning
world is beautiful
from a distance.

Oracle

Before humans began suppressing fires, wildfires were part of a natural, regenerative cycle. In the Mountain West, every 30 years or so a fire would come through, burning up duff and detritus and smaller trees that, if left to grow, would crowd the forest and deprive the understory of the light it needs to flourish. Forests would be renewed, the ashes of the burned matter nurturing new life.

Many of our forests are now out of balance. For more than half a century, we suppressed all the fires—big and small—and forests have grown crowded and dense. When they burn, they burn hot and destructively, raging through the overstory and decimating ecosystems. As we work to restore our forests, we must also contend with wildfires that threaten everything in their paths.

It could be that some aspect of your life—career, family, health, love life—is out of balance and risking catastrophe. You need to restore balance, and with it, resiliency, so that if catastrophe does strike, you will survive.

You probably will need support, and chances are those who know and love you may not know you need it. You may have to level with them so that they understand, and you may have to ask for help directly. And if everything burns to the ground, know that new life will push up through the ashes. While nothing will be as before, the new terrain will be rich with possibility.

37. The Council

Our chairs—municipal. Tacked in leather and richly
padded but easily adjustable, designed for the endless
replacement of asses. We linger past term limits, eye
the patina of each other's nameplates. We amend

the past over free creamer. We are called
forefathers, thugs, toxic like the groundwater
and stunted like the crops. We prefer puppets
of the evil fuckwit and advocates for orphans.

Our collective wit is unsparing and we govern
accordingly. Which is to say within the traditions
established during times of prosperity. Which is
funny. Appreciated by several regular attendees

of monthly town meetings despite their ignored
petitions. What is left to save? A desiccated High
Street. A ghosted shore. They haunt their own histories
to keep from disappearing. We just want new chairs.

Oracle

It's easy to believe that those who hold positions of power do so because they are smart or wise or judicious. That they gained their position by earning the respect of others, that they have learned from years of experience. But we all know inept people who find their way to power through other paths, ranging from deceit to artful manipulation to luck.

It can be scary to think the people in charge are no more qualified than you are—their logic flawed and their decisions faulty. It is risky, however, to dismiss this possibility, especially when the decisions they make impact your health or happiness or livelihood.

It's possible that there is an authority in your life—boss, coach, counselor, doctor, financial advisor, government representative—whom you trust has your best interests in mind. And in many cases they sincerely do. But it could be that they aren't the sages and scholars that you think they are. They are fallible. And if they stumble, they can take you down, too. It may be time for you to think for yourself, do your research (using reputable sources), question, disagree, rebel. Then assume authority over your own choices. You are more qualified than you think.

38. The Pine

First the seed. The cone
it came from. The hand that buried
it. The story inside. Story of root
and stem, rock and loam. Of hollow,
smoke and storm. Hundreds
of years

        of story. Aiming for
sky, stretching to water. Voices
chorus, each needle's rustle
and thrum. *The story is difficult
to hear on still evenings.
The story is difficult to decipher
in the wind.* But

        listen. The nuthatch
sings it. The squirrel skitters its code
along thin branches. The rain carries
the story to the streams. Needles fall
and the soil clings to every

        word. You
know this story. Remember how
you belong. The first time you heard
its rustle, the last time its cadence
shadowed your pulse.

Oracle

The 21st-century relationship between people and nature is often presented as discordant, at odds: nature is a resource for people to use, so protecting nature impacts our ability and right to exploit it. This model is premised on the assumption that people are *apart from* nature, not *a part of* nature. But for thousands of years, people and nature have been two component parts of a symbiotic, reciprocal system: we take care of land and water and they sustain us in return.

If you are feeling lethargic, incomplete, unfulfilled, it could be that you've lost your connection to nature. Reconnecting could be as simple as a walk in a nearby park, finding a tree to sit under, or stepping outside to gaze at the clouds. The physical and mental benefits of returning to nature are well-documented and include everything from improved memory and concentration to increased happiness, relaxation and vitamin D production. And it doesn't hurt that the more time you spend in nature, the more likely you are to take care of it as nature, in return, takes care of you.

39. The Freeze

Nothing gives. Branches, gears,
fingers, vows—all ripe
for breaking. The ground
rips beneath boot tread
shaped to cut. To move
is to scrape even
the air, molecules yanked
from their brittle

hibernation. This town
is used to time
slowed to still,
like the wolves holding
their crouch before
the pounce, then

forgetting. It's understandable,
feeling like the only
living thing, but the lake
moves as a ghost does, only
at the corner
of your eye. Slabs

of ice creep to the shore,
shards pile on the shattered

surface. A glimmer of water
seeps to the surface
and spreads, beckoned
by sunlight too feeble
to discern the living
from the dead.

Oracle

Whether it's a nap or a longer period of dormancy, everyone needs to shut down and let time move on without us. While we all know this, some of us have a harder time stopping. Producing, consuming, receiving, nurturing, thinking, moving. Maybe we are afraid that if we stop, we stop *being*. That the association between sleep and death is more than metaphorical.

But rest is not the opposite of being. It is the endurance of being. Like water beneath a frozen lake, life teems within us. The brain locks down new information and clears waste. Nerve cells shift and communicate. The body repairs damage, restores energy, and releases hormones and proteins that we need to function.

It could be simply that you need more rest. Get some sleep. Meditate. Let your injury heal. But perhaps it goes deeper than that. It could be that you are afraid that if you stop doing then you'll start to fade. That your identity is tied up in your productivity. But the opposite is true. Constant doing without reprieve will wear you away. It could be that what is missing from your life—what you need to be whole—are periods of stillness and quiet. Give yourself permission to solely exist.

40. The Baker

Heat the least of it.

        Honey from domed recesses of a hollowed mountain.

                The animalness thrumming, bucket warm.

                        Butter sometimes. Eggs.

                        Richness only a body can give.

Hands deep (*lebkuchen, struffoli, baklava, mézeskalács, chebakia, dabo*)

in dough.

                Everywhere and Elsewhere: from the living into us.

Oracle

The Baker symbolizes abundance: bread baskets and shelves filled with rich and delicious cakes and pastries. It isn't just the profusion of both life-sustaining bread and luxurious treats that signifies plenty, it's also the bounty of resources all that food implies: lush fields of grain, access to spices and sugar, animals to produce butter and honey and eggs.

Archetypal representations of bakers are usually plump, as if they are made of the same dough they knead and shape and transform, personifying abundance—a benevolent creator who honors the limitless giving of life from the earth.

Perhaps you are at a point in your life where you are able to transform your abundance into something to send back into the world: a community service, a financial contribution, or volunteering your expertise where it can have impact. Even if that creative giving can't be sustained, imagine what you can transform through a single act of generosity.

41. The Moon

If the moon could feel pity it would not
        pity the town of Elsewhere. If the moon
could help it would not
        help. If the moon could provide guidance
or empathy it would, instead, practice the cruel art of
        withholding. So far
away the moon can barely be bothered. So ancient, the moon
        knows even a few words of encouragement (which
        costs the moon nothing) would arrive
too late, future generations puzzled by her mumblings,
        gazing up at passions obscured
by the bend of space and time. The moon offers only
    the illusion of proximity, pulling at tides
        and blood cycles,
            saying this is something.
        This is more than enough.

Oracle

It's hard to believe that something that spends its entire existence orbiting us could be indifferent to our fate. But with each turn around the earth, the moon is also distancing itself from us at a rate of 1.5 inches a year (so says science). The moon is constant, rising and setting each day, but it is also inconstant, the time of its rise always changing, its phases and movements dependent on the earth's spinning and tilted orbit around the sun. Beautiful and mystifying, the moon is attributed to both feminine power and provoking the monstrous. It's complicated. And confusing.

Perhaps you are in a period of confusion, looking for answers where none exists. Or you may be feeling ambivalent or uncertain, not trusting your instincts or senses. Though unsettling, these periods of fluctuation and limbo can be a time for introspection and inaction—learning and perceiving instead of deciding and doing. And like the moon, you will pass through this phase soon enough, and soon enough you will pass through it again.

42. The Judge

I want nachos with habaneros
smoking.

       I want double-barreled whiskey
from a bottle in the street.

       I want Sheriff
in my bed, my mouth raising heat
in her windburned cheeks.

       I want robes
woven from corruption and cattle thieves,
chocolate and deer shot, the ace
of clubs missing and no one reaching
up my sleeve.

       Give me a dismissive gesture as my
signature tic.

       Give me outrage and spittle, a high
pitched cackle, an obvious agenda and a dark,
gilled thing for a pet.

       Give me dynamite, cough
syrup, a dive to the bottom, pull the boat down
in my wake.

       Say you don't dream.

                                          Say you
    believe your own story.

                            Say you want nothing
  from me.

Oracle

Discretion, propriety, reserve, restraint, tact, temperance, moderation, self-control, dignity, discipline. All necessary. All excellent tools for productive relationships, professional success, parenting, social networking, communication, crisis management, and a half-dozen other adult activities and goals. Also, all overrated and kinda boring.

Some of our relationships call for letting go, letting down barriers, letting our whole selves show, including the messy, sloppy, crazy, wanton, improper bits. Especially if we are working to build authentic connections and trust. This might be hard for you to do right now. Trust that others will not only accept—and even embrace—those parts of yourself that you are less inclined to reveal, but also that they will feel encouraged to reveal themselves to you in return.

43. The Spring

Where water
    is resurrected

Where bear pause and drink
    and coyote drink, and pronghorn.
    Where the last puma spotted
    the first wolf, where a deer skeleton
    was dragged twenty yards into the woods

Where the curved wall crumbled into a slope
    of stone once gathered and stacked
    by someone no one can recall

Where the wild iris flourish, and the woods'
    rose, its hips after blossom
    for the robin, the thrasher, the white
    crowned sparrow

Where Gloríana wandered when Bodi abandoned
    Elsewhere

Where the small ones gather, itching
    or mud and water bugs

Where the water bubbles up pellucid, tastes
    of limestone—scoured and intemerate

Where the ripples, veined
    with shadow, settle into light

Oracle

Springs are the result of rainwater or snow melt soaking deep into the earth, often becoming fortified with minerals as water moves through rock fractures on its way back to the surface. At some springs, the journey can take hundreds or even thousands of years, which means that some spring water hasn't seen the Earth's surface since well before the industrial revolution and is untouched by contaminants.

There is something inside you that you have kept below the surface. Something generative and sustaining: creative drive, fierce love, risk taking. It could be a part of you kept buried to protect yourself, or a part of you stowed away because you felt like you had no use for it in the life you are living. Perhaps that something—transformed by its time underground—is bubbling up, soon to emerge, and you will need to make room for it at the surface. More likely, you are at a place where you could really use your subterranean resource, and it's time to tap into it and let it flow.

44. The Storyteller

If I say that I am damaged
would that be a story
I tell myself? The garden

turns brown no matter
how much or how little
I water. But to claim
responsibility for everything
that fails to thrive
can be a symptom

of egocentrism. I tell
myself I am not that
powerful, but guilt is more
powerful than the story
I tell myself. *Tell
yourself a different
story* the Council says, not
to be controlling but
to encourage better

outcomes. I do my
best to nurture
vegetation, small
children, my career,
and intimate
relationships, but sometimes
I do the opposite. Shiva
is the creator

and the destroyer.
I don't know how he
manages the balance
without cultivating

a horrible reputation.
What we tell ourselves
often starts with what
we are told. Or our stories
can't survive the scrutiny

of collective belief
systems. Or maybe
I am weaker than
most, easily permeated
by commentary. In
that way I have come
to distrust my stories,

even the one with the wolf.
Sometimes it gets so
close, I can smell it.
I can see its fur
bristling, the air
changing as its muscles
tense, lips draw
back from its teeth.
This is a story I tell

myself I tell myself,
my hands already
covering my throat.

Telling a story doesn't
make it true, but
sometimes truth is
what a story makes.

Oracle

We are often our own best obstacles (or our own worst enemies). Nothing can stop us faster or more forcefully than ourselves. Who hasn't told themselves that they are hopeless? Stupid. Unlovable. Unlikeable. Not good enough. Talentless. Unattractive. A bad child. A bad parent. Resourceless. Luckless. Worthy of disdain. This isn't about a lack of agency. This is agency turned against ourselves.

Even if some of the stories we tell ourselves are based in truth, *we can change the truth by changing the story*. If you tell yourself that you will never be successful, then there is no chance you'll ever succeed. But what if you tweak the story to you haven't succeeded *yet*? What, then, are the new possible futures you've created?

It is time to re-examine the stories you tell yourself. You may need a new story, or a fresh take on an old story. And let that story create a truth that serves you well.

45. The Trickster (Gloriana III)

                  Do not come with me to the water
rocks   slick and hidden   shift
   beneath the weight   of even the small
     child   who drifts   like ghosts   you could
break an ankle or   worse   long dead
      barnacles edged like   boning knives
        will slice a tendon   no telling
       what blood will bring
    from the depths   run
      when the child   runs   thunderheads
love   the lake gather   and swell
   like a blister above   a bruise   call
creatures   to the surface   do not
      come with me I   cannot
protect   you no one   can save
anyone else I   can perhaps   tell you
   the path   map   the sandy-bottomed shallows
  what to give the child   the others
   who watch   over her   I could send
     you   with my   blessing
      the water loves   me   you would
not believe   the offerings   I've made

Oracle

The ambivalent, ambiguous, shape-shifting, situation-inverting, convention-defying, chaos-embodying trickster messes with our heads. Br'er Rabbit, Anansi, Coyote, Loki, Puss-in-Boots, Puck, the Pink Panther, Jack Sparrow—all tricksters. You may have a trickster in your life. One way to tell is if—when describing the person or your relationship with them—you use the phrase, "It's complicated."

A relationship with a trickster is similar to having the rug pulled out beneath you only to discover another rug and suspecting it will be also be pulled away. But perhaps you stand on it because you love it. Or you find it exciting. Or the rug is a magic rug. Or against your better judgment you believe that, for you, the rug will stay put. A trickster will turn your world upside down, invite you to question values, tempt you to thumb your nose at rules, all of which can be wonderful—if destabilizing—experiences.

But sometimes it's hard to tell the difference between a trickster and an ass. Their actions are often similar on the surface even if intent is wildly different. A friend or lover who lets you down repeatedly can seem to be—and often sell themselves as—sly tricksters defying expectations and pushing you out of your comfort zone. While you may welcome the occasional trickster, don't waste your time or emotional energy on chronic jerks. It is a hard-earned skill to be able to tell the difference, and it may be a skill that you need to put into action.

46. The Torch Singer

Oh sugar
mine. Oh overripe
fruit. Oh honeypot
ant near bursting. Oh
thirst. Oh shiver
in the heat, front
porch in shadow,
a body blocking
the sun. The one

who runs returns
holding an outdated
map. He can't get
away and he won't
stay, the space
between us a high
street, so many mindless
exchanges. I sing

the low notes mostly,
nights the VFW has
open mic. Lower
than growl, lower
than rumble, so
low my call is the one
thing requited,
and the shudder beneath
the lake sends waves
beyond the shore. Oh

depths. Oh dark
one. Oh bottomless
love. Oh territory. Oh
there before us, there
after we are gone.

Oracle

While many people do eventually find the person (or people) who can make them happy for an extended period of time, or even until death, most relationships end, and end badly. If we're lucky, with no ill will. If we're unlucky, with legal complications or potential harm. So, the unrequited instances of love, though painful, may save us from more severe consequences.

At the same time, the accumulation of sentiment resulting from unrequited love—not unlike the buildup of electrical charges in a thundercloud before lightning strikes—must be discharged. While some outlets are unproductive (like resentment) or even dangerous (like stalking), pent-up emotional energy may be directed to creative endeavors that—if not worth the heartache—at least softens it a bit.

Think of all the beautiful torch songs that the heartbroken have created out of their despair. The paintings and poems and sculpture. Write something, sing something, choreograph a dance, pick up an instrument, a piece of clay, a paintbrush. The love that you generate is yours to do with what you will.

47. The Ghost

You may have heard the world is quiet now. So still a forgotten
scarf—fluttering in the breeze then settling—is enough
of an omen. Then an aspen
leaf, fallen and brittle, skitters across your path. Wheels
on an upturned scooter spin on their trucks. The air electric
with static, particles dying for motion. Absence. But the world

is not quiet, only *difficult to hear* *on still evenings,*
difficult to decipher *in the wind.* Listen. It teems.
As if with excitable children uncertain of expectations,
joy and panic in the same repeated gestures. What remains

refuses to be buried. How can you not feel the impending
surge, like a dam collapsing. You may think
the reckoning will not reach you, that I speak
from Elsewhere. But you are from Elsewhere, too.

Oracle

While your problems and challenges may seem overwhelming at times, they are no match for you. They are small in comparison to your fortitude and resilience. Just look back at some of your most difficult struggles. How much space in your life do they now occupy? While our past struggles may always be a part of us, that part continues to shrink as time passes. And when new struggles take their place, we understand that we can overcome them, too.

There are larger challenges, however, that affect us even as we dismiss them as irrelevant to our lives. Or we may think them too large to do anything about. Or as issues better tackled by someone else—someone with more time or expertise or knowledge. But the truth is that the same resources you draw on to conquer your personal struggles are needed elsewhere. You are necessary. You can help save the world. You have more to offer than you think.

48. The Farmer

I'm not much for mystics and historians. They twist
  a fine plait of past and future. Wreck the easy truth
    of things with their threads tying one thing
  to the next, knots and tangles suddenly part of the story.
    Truth is I fallowed the back fields because
      the soil wasn't good. Never should have
cleared that stretch of land in the first place. Downstream
from the leachate pit, every growing thing stunted
      and small. Let those woods creep in and claim what is
    theirs. I'm not scared. Better to be swallowed
up than picked over by crows. There's more
    than one way to be left behind.

Oracle

Data and facts can be black and white, but truth is never absolute. Truth is part fact, part perception, part perspective, part (faulty) memory, part belief, part desire. There is a lot—perhaps too much—emphasis on speaking one's truth, an intentional blocking out of opinions and perceptions that don't align with—or that threaten—our own. Collective truths seem rare, especially in this age of segmented media, bias, and spin.

And while it is important to know what we know, to refuse to be gaslit, to sidestep the steamrollers and to resist propaganda, it's also important to stay open to new information and ideas. Because what if we're wrong?

Completely wrong or wrong in part or wrong to a small degree? Who has not been 100% sure only to find out they were 100% mistaken.

Perhaps you are clinging to a truth that needs to be re-examined or fine-tuned. Perhaps your truth needs some corroboration, input from someone else or from a source of information you would normally not consult. Personal truths can be isolating. By opening your truth to others, you also open yourself up to intimacy and connection. To evolution and growth. Which may be the things your truth is missing.

49. The Woods

Beneath the overstory. Beneath the upstart
firs and aspens. Beneath shards of filtered light suspending
tufts and seeds, pieces of carapace, particles

of rot. Beneath webs and nests and hollows,
birdsong and rustles. Beneath the white moths, their mad
fluttering paths among the yarrow. Beneath

paintbrush and monkshood, cheatgrass
and brome. Beneath moss and rocks and the fallen
log, insects churning its insides to

marrow. Beneath the burdock and nettle
roots Gloríana unearths for cures. An accumulation.
A history of histories layered in detritus

and duff. Compressed. And the past
thins. Bones linger. Bits of those who came
before. What they held. What

they poisoned. Leaching
to the surface. Refusing to stay
down.

Oracle
Recent science has revealed a symbiotic relationship between trees and microorganisms in the soil that create a (kind of) communication network connecting all the trees in the vicinity. Mast years—the

phenomenon of trees seemingly coordinating mass production of fruit or nuts—may be partly attributed to this underground network of roots sending messages through microorganisms to their neighbors. Which is to say that much of a tree's story unfolds beneath the surface.

Which could also be said of people. It could be that someone close to you is acting in a way you don't understand, and it is affecting you and your relationship. You probably need to stop focusing on the surface (behavior) and dig beneath to understand their motivations. Or perhaps you need to pay more attention to your interior. It's possible that your heart and gut and soul (in whatever way you define soul) have been having a conversation but are not having much luck involving your mind. Listen in. You may find an answer there.

50. The Sun

*No gold but honey no
coin but corn. No fortune
but horizon ten minutes
before dawn. Lemon
pith, peach swell, melon
in dirt, songbird, dragon
fly, columbine, goat. No
shadow but shades no
storm no smoke. No jewel
but cherry no red but
heart. Glint from the mine
shaft, shimmer in
the woods. No drink
but juice from the red
bright fruit.*

Oracle

Joy does not come from reason or logic. Abundance can be unearned. You may work hard for good fortune and happiness but not achieve them, only to be showered by random blessings and windfalls when you least expect it. We make our own luck, but it's foolish not to acknowledge the external factors at play that can be stronger than our will.

There's no telling how the universe works, how it balances out or doesn't. Sometimes circumstances come together in incredibly beneficent ways that we could never orchestrate on our own and would never have planned or expected. It could be that you are currently experiencing a period of good fortune or that it is impending. It could also be that you just really, really need some luck right now. It is coming. The important thing is not to squander it. Use it to fuel your fire and burn brightly while you can.

Anywhere but Elsewhere: Coda

Elsewhere? It still exists. Despite the shuttered factory, the row crops returning to wild grasses, the mined-out mountain that disappeared from the horizon. Elsewhere is, by definition, a multitude. Every place that is not here is Elsewhere. It is endless. Endlessly open to invention. Endless opportunities for tragedy. Endless opportunities for joy. But once you choose—or even imagine—Elsewhere, it is no longer Elsewhere. It is There. And you are never There. You are never Elsewhere. You are here. For better or worse. Make it better. Here.

Acknowledgments

I am grateful to the editors of the following magazines and journals that have published several of the pieces included in *The Elsewhere Oracle*, sometimes in earlier versions: *Dark Onus Lit, Glint, Grimsy, LIT, Midnight Chem, Lammergeier Journal.*

So much appreciation and gratitude to all the amazing folks of the Good Hart Artist Residency, especially Bill and Sue Klco, for the space and time to write across the street from your beautiful piece of Lake Michigan, and for feeding my body and soul. So much of Good Hart is in Elsewhere.

A big thank you to Martha Silano and Hyejung Kook for your grace and generosity as you nudged me through revisions.

Selah Saterstrom, Kristen E. Nelson, Teresa Carmody, Megan Kaminski, Hoa Nguyen, and Hillary Leftwich—you helped me to find the crossroads where writing and divination meet. I am in awe of your practice and insight.

Priscilla Gonzalez, your artwork is still my favorite among the masterpieces. Thank you for jumpstarting the deck.

Hezekiah Goode, that line about the shooter in the tower is so good I had to steal it.

Many museums make great works of art available for everyone's creative use through open access. I discovered many artists whose work enthralled me, such as Odilon Redon and Jeanne Bieruma Oosting. It was a gift to explore endless archives.

To all my colleagues at The Nature Conservancy, especially in Colorado, when I write about nature, I write from your work, wisdom, and passion. Thank you for sharing a mission and a vision.

Mark and Marky, remember that time years ago when Elsewhere was only an idea and we were driving to meet Joey at the arcade, and you, John, and Henry helped me brainstorm archetypes for the arcana? I remember.

Mom and Wil, I wrote so much of this lounging in the paradise cage. Thank you for a place and space to write.

John, my compass. I could not find my way to—and through—Elsewhere without you.

Henry, you are my best. When I divine the future, I see you.

Art Attributions

All artworks included in *The Elsewhere Oracle* are either in the public domain, publicly available for commercial use under the Creative Commons Zero (CC0) license, or used with permission by the artist. Sources include open access/public domain collections from the Art Institute of Chicago, the Cleveland Museum of Art, the Clark Art Institute, the Cooper Hewitt Smithsonian Design Museum, The Metropolitan Museum of Art, the National Gallery of Art, the National Museum of Asian Art, the National Portrait Gallery, The New York Public Library, rawpixel, the Rijksmuseum, the Smithsonian American Art Museum, and the Smithsonian Institute.

1. The Factory: *How the Pipes are Hung* by Joseph Pennell (1867–1926). Smithsonian American Art Museum, Renwick Gallery.
2. The Gunsmith: *Revolver* (ca.1942) by Elizabeth Johnson. National Gallery of Art.
3. The Mountain: *Mont Sainte-Victoire and the Viaduct of the Arc River Valley* (ca. 1882–85) by Paul Cézanne. The Metropolitan Museum of Art.
4. The Barkeep: *The Wine Glass* (1858) by James McNeill Whistler. National Museum of Asian Art.
5. The Lake: *Carter Lake* (ca. 1880) by Willian Louis Sontag. Cooper Hewitt, Smithsonian Design Institute.
6. The Orphan: *Head of a Child (Emmanual)* (1898) by Charles Angrand. Art Institute of Chicago.
7. The Ceremony: *A Nymph Bathing, Moonlight* (1890–1900) by Theodore Roussel. Art Institute of Chicago.

8. The Confectioner: *Höllandischer Cacao* (1897) by Johann Georg van Caspel. Rijksmuseum.

9. The Soot: *The Forest in Winter at Sunset* (1846–67) by Théodore Rousseau. The Metropolitan Museum of Art.

10. The Gardener: *Decorative Study: Woman with Sunflowers* (1892/1898) by Aubrey Vincent Beardsley. Art Institute of Chicago.

11. The Well: *The Well* (2021) by Priscilla Gonzalez.

12. The Healer: *Ville-d'Avray* (1870) by Camille Corot. The Metropolitan Museum of Art.

13. The Ossuary: *Skull* (1520) by Hans Wechtlin I. National Gallery of Art.

14. The Hunter: *Campfire, Adirondacks* (ca. 1892) by Winslow Homer. Smithsonian Institute.

15. The High Street: *Street in Sainte-Adresse* (1867) by Claude Monet. Clark Art Institute.

16. The Immigrant: *The Immigrant* (2021) by Priscilla Gonzalez.

17. The Almanac: *Almanac for 1789* (1789). Cooper Hewitt, Smithsonian Design Institute.

18. The Hermit: *Woodlands at the Hermitage* (1879) by Camille Passero. Art Institute of Chicago.

19. The Wolves: *Woman with a torch, child and wolf* (1904) by Richard Roland Holst. Rijksmuseum.

20. The Doctor: *Doctor Charles Doolittle Walcott* (1913) by Ossip Perelma. Smithsonian American Art Museum.

21. The Artifact: *Art industriel: boites et ustensiles de toilette from Histoire de l'art égyptien* (1878) by Émile Prisse d'Avennes. The New York Public Library.

22. The Seer: *The Penitent Magdalen* (ca. 1640) by Georges de La Tour. The Metropolitan Museum of Art.

23. The Storm: *Weymouth Bay* (1830) by David Lucas. The Metropolitan Museum of Art.

24. The Counselor: *Dance of Death: The Councillor* (ca. 1526) by Hans Holbein. Cleveland Museum of Art.

25. The Menu: *Hors d'oeuvres dishes and savouries* (1861) from *Mrs. Beeton's Book of Household Management*. rawpixel.

26. The Robber Baron: *Melville Elijah Stone* by Carlo de Fornaro. National Portrait Gallery.

27. The Compass: *Ship's Compass* (ca. 1937) by Magnus S. Fossum. National Gallery of Art.

28. The Archive: *Library of Winchester College* (ca. 1816) by Frederick MacKenzie. Art Institute of Chicago.

29. The Sheriff: *Portrait of a Young Woman* (ca. 1690) by Aert de Gelder. Art Institute of Chicago.

30. The Warren: *Rabbits at full moon* (1920–30) by Ohara Koson. Rijksmuseum.

31. The Gravekeeper: *O Grave, where is thy Victory?* (1892) by Jan Toorop. Rijksmuseum.

32. The Plague: *The Sick Child* (1894) by Edvard Munch. Art Institute of Chicago.

33. The Teacher: *Teacher*, from the Occupations for Women series (N166) for Old Judge and Dogs Head Cigarettes (1887), Issued by Goodwin & Company. Art Institute of Chicago.

34. The Drought: *Krimpscheuren* (1979) by Diederik Kraaijpoel. Rijksmuseum.

35. The Meadow: *Sahurs Meadows in Morning Sun* (1894) by Alfred Sisley. The Metropolitan Museum of Art.

36. The Wildfire: *The Prairie on Fire* (1827) by Alvan Fisher. Art Institute of Chicago.

37. The Council: *On the Street* (ca. 1914) by Ernst Ludwig Kirchner. Cleveland Museum of Art.

38. The Pine: *Pine Tree* (no date) by Sandow. The Metropolitan Museum of Art.

39. The Freeze: *Winter Sunset* (ca. 1890) by Birge Harrison. Smithsonian American Art Museum, Renwick Gallery.

40. The Baker: Bread (1911) from *The Grocer's Encyclopedia*. rawpixel.

41. The Moon: *Sheepyard, Moonlight* (1906) by Horatio Walker. Smithsonian American Art Museum.

42. The Judge: *Judge Hand Puppet (*ca. 1936) by Beverly Chichester. National Gallery of Art.

43. The Spring: *The Source* (1862) by Gustave Courbet. The Metropolitan Museum of Art.

44. The Storyteller: *The Book of Light* (1893) by Odilon Redon. National Gallery of Art.

45. The Trickster: *Heks* (1626) by Jan van de Velde. Rijksmuseum.

46. The Torch Singer: *The Torch Singer* (2021) by Priscilla Gonzalez.

47. The Ghost: *The Watching Eyes* (1935) by Jeanne Bieruma Oosting. Rijksmuseum.

48. The Farmer: *Interior of a Peasant Hut* (ca. 1882) by Jozef Israëls. Rijksmuseum.

49. The Woods: *Autumn, a Wood Path* (1876) by Sanford Robinson Gifford. Cleveland Museum of Art.

50. The Sun: *Red Sunset on the Dnieper (Dnipro)* (1905–08) by Arkhip Ivanovich Kuindzhi. The Metropolitan Museum of Art.

Michele Battiste is the author of four books of poems, including *Waiting for the Wreck to Burn* (Trio House Press, 2019), which won the Louise Bogan Award for Artistic Merit and Excellence. Michele's work has appeared in several publications, including *American Poetry Review*, *American Book Review*, *The Rumpus*, and *Women's Studies Quarterly*. Born and raised in New York, she lives in Colorado where she works to protect nature, hikes the foothills with her dog Juju, and writes poems, stories, and divinations.